Ladybird Readers

Roald Dahl

T0368809

The Magic Finger
Activity Book

Based on the original title by Roald Dahl
Illustrated by Quentin Blake

Written by Hazel Geatches
Song lyrics on page 16 written by Wardour Studios

 Singing * Reading Speaking Critical thinking

 Spelling Writing Listening *

*To complete these activities, listen to tracks 2, 3, and 4 of the Reader audio download available at **www.ladybirdeducation.co.uk**

1 Match the words to the pictures.

1 stick

2 nest

3 deer

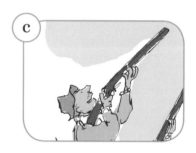

4 leaves

5 gun

6 bite

2 Find the words.

tnee(deer)apgunpedoonestrebitelngshootestleavese

1

deer

2

3

4

5

6

3 Who said this?

Philip

Mrs. Winter

Mrs. Gregg

Mr. Gregg

William

1 "Look! Someone is in our garden!" .... Philip ....

2 "There's a duck in my bed!" ....

3 "Where are we going to sleep?" ....

4 "We can build a nest!" ....

5 "Stand up and spell cat." ....

Look and read. Circle the correct words.

1

a leaves

b stick

c pieces

2

a hungry

b windy

c angry

3

a nest

b next

c best

4

a three

b tree

c toy

5 Listen, and put a ✓ by the correct sentences.

1 a "We can build a nest!" ✓

   b "We can't build a nest!" ☐

2 a "Don't bring lots of sticks and leaves." ☐

   b "Now, bring lots of sticks and leaves." ☐

3 a "We'll fly into our house through an open window and get some biscuits." ☐

   b "We'll fly into our nest and get some biscuits." ☐

4 a "We can eat apples! Come on!" ☐

   b "We can't eat apples! Come on!" ☐

5 a "Our two little children aren't here with us." ☐

   b "Our two little children are here with us." ☐

6 a "I will not break the guns into small pieces." ☐

   b "I will break the guns into small pieces." ☐

 *To complete this activity, listen to track 2 of the Reader audio download available at www.ladybirdeducation.co.uk

6 Look and read. Write *T* (true) or *F* (false).

1 There was a duck in the bathroom. ....F....

2 There was a duck in the kitchen. ....

3 The duck in the kitchen was cleaning. ....

4 The duck in the kitchen had a magic finger. ....

5 One duck had a gun. ....

6 There was a duck in William's bed. ....

7 The duck in the bed was reading. ....

8 A duck was playing with Philip's toy cars. ....

1  Mrs. Winter turned around . . . and she had a **head!** / (**tail!**)

2  He did not have **a nose** / **arms** —he had wings!

3  She was also very small now, and she had **windows,** / **wings,** too.

4  The ducks were as big as **men,** / **the house,** and they had arms, not wings.

5  "Don't cry," Mr. Gregg said. "We can **grow** / **build** a nest!"

6  "Look at that duck in our **kitchen!"** / **garden!"** cried Mrs. Gregg.

8 Look, match, and write the words.

1 fli — es

2 sti — ves

3 tou — ches

4 lea — oots

5 sh — ger

6 fin — ck

1 flies   **2** _____

3 _____   **4** _____

5 _____   **6** _____

9 Look at the pictures.
Put a ✓ in the correct boxes.

1

a hat ☐

b hot ✓

2

a hand ☐

b and ☐

3

a hed ☐

b head ☐

4

a dear ☐

b deer ☐

5

a ear ☐

b ere ☐

6

a toys ☐

b boys ☐

10 Work with a friend.
Ask and answer questions about the picture.

1 Can the Greggs fly?

Yes, they can.

2 Can the Greggs sleep in their house?

3 Can the Greggs make a nest?

4 Can Philip and William play with their toys?

11 Look at the pictures. Which picture is different? Put a ✓ in the correct boxes and write the sentences below. 📖 ✏️ ❓

> He is not an animal. They do not have guns.
> They are not happy. They do not have wings.

1 ⓐ ✓ ⓑ ☐ ⓒ ☐

He is not an animal.

2 ⓐ ☐ ⓑ ☐ ⓒ ☐

3 ⓐ ☐ ⓑ ☐ ⓒ ☐

4 ⓐ ☐ ⓑ ☐ ⓒ ☐

12 **Draw a picture of Mr. Gregg. Read the questions and write about Mr. Gregg.**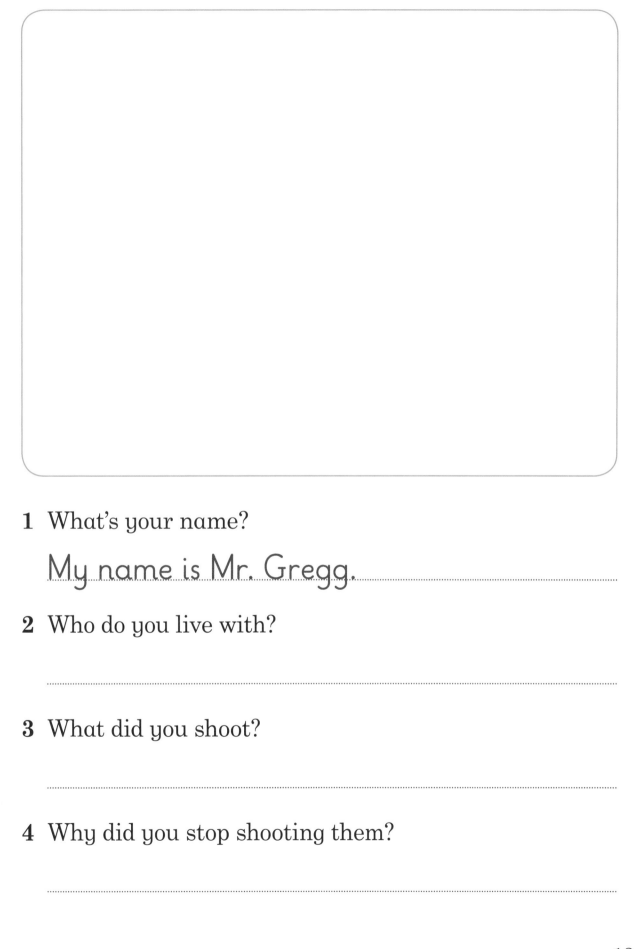

1 What's your name?

   My name is Mr. Gregg.

2 Who do you live with?

3 What did you shoot?

4 Why did you stop shooting them?

13 Listen, and write a—f. *

"What happened?" I asked.

Philip and William told me their story. "Look at our nest!" they said. "We slept there last night."

"We built it," said Mr. Gregg, happily. "Every stick—and we have changed our name. We are not the Gregg family. We are the Egg family, because we love birds now!"

44

45

1 "We are the Egg family,
because we love birds now!" ......f....

2 "We are not the Gregg family." ....

3 "We slept there last night." ....

4 "What happened?" ....

5 "We have changed our name." ....

6 "Look at our nest!" ....

*To complete this activity, listen to track 3 of the Reader audio download available at **www.ladybirdeducation.co.uk**

14 Work with a friend. Help the ducks catch the Gregg family. Use the words in the box. ◯

turn right   go straight   turn left   go to the end

Turn right. Then, turn left . . .

15 Sing the song. *

I have a magic finger.
It feels strange when I'm mad.
Things start to happen then . . .
They're sometimes good and sometimes bad!

It happened in school.
I was asked to spell.
I thought from my answer that I had done well.
The teacher said I was wrong, that was that—
I pointed my finger, now she is a cat!

It happened next door.
The Greggs liked to use guns.
I pointed my finger at Mr. Gregg and his sons.
They all became birds and lived in a nest.
Then they stopped shooting the ducks,
and it was all for the best!

I have a magic finger.
It feels strange when I'm mad.
Things start to happen then . . .
They're sometimes good and sometimes bad!

*To complete this activity, listen to track 4 of the Reader audio download available at **www.ladybirdeducation.co.uk**